I0483054

Occupational Safety and Health Act of 1970
"To assure safe and healthful working conditions for working men and women; by authorizing enforcement of the standards developed under the Act; by assisting and encouraging the States in their efforts to assure safe and healthful working conditions; by providing for research, information, education, and training in the field of occupational safety and health."

This information will be made available to sensory-impaired individuals upon request. Voice phone: (202) 693-1999; teletypewriter (TTY) number: 1-877-889-5627.

Cover photo: Elena Finizo, Braintree, Massachusetts Area Office.

Solutions for the Prevention of Musculoskeletal Injuries in Foundries

**Occupational Safety and Health Administration
U.S. Department of Labor**

OSHA 3465-08
2012

U.S. Department of Labor
Hilda L. Solis, Secretary of Labor

OSHA would like to thank the following foundries for their hospitality, time, and effort during OSHA's site visits to the plants: Neenah Foundry, ThyssenKrupp Waupaca Foundry, Brillion Iron Works, Roloff Manufacturing, Manitowoc Grey Iron Foundry, and Wisconsin Aluminum Foundry in Wisconsin, as well as the Clow Valve Foundry in Iowa. OSHA greatly appreciates these foundries' cooperation and willingness to share with the Agency information on the improvements made in their plants, the statements from the workers and the management, and their comments on the draft publication. OSHA's National Office is grateful to the OSHA Area Office in Appleton, Wisconsin and the Wisconsin Health Consultation Program for their participation in the design of this publication and their contributions to the Agency's efforts to reduce musculoskeletal injuries in the workplace.

Contents

EXECUTIVE SUMMARY

Many proactive initiatives undertaken by the foundry industry, including establishing ergonomic processes, incorporating ergonomic principles into new projects, and conducting facility walkthroughs to identify injury risks have resulted in a reduction in worker injuries and illnesses (1). Employees working in foundries are often exposed to ergonomics-related injury risks, such as lifting heavy items, bending, reaching overhead, pushing and pulling heavy loads, working in awkward body postures, and performing the same or similar tasks repetitively (1). The physically demanding tasks performed during foundry operations may be responsible for the musculoskeletal disorders (MSDs) developed by workers in this industry. Foundry workers have higher MSD injury rates than workers in general industry and construction (2).

Although many ergonomics-related risk factors exist in foundries, this industry has found ways to make the work less stressful through ergonomic solutions. The successful efforts of some foundries to address this important issue provide a sufficient basis for replicating these actions to better protect foundry workers.

This publication provides recommendations for foundries to help increase employer and worker awareness of ergonomics-related risk factors, alleviate muscle fatigue, increase productivity, and reduce the number and severity of work-related MSDs.

In developing these guidelines, OSHA visited six foundries in Wisconsin (Neenah Foundry, Waupaca Foundry, Brillion Iron Works, Roloff Manufacturing, Manitowoc Grey Iron Foundry, and Wisconsin Aluminum Foundry) and the Clow Valve Foundry in Iowa to review the foundries' ergonomic programs, observe existing ergonomic practices in action, talk with managers, interview workers and union members, and take pictures of the engineering solutions. Whenever possible, OSHA also obtained photos of foundry tasks prior to implementation of the ergonomic solutions. Moreover, some photos were retrieved from PowerPoint presentations designed by the foundries visited. In addition, OSHA reviewed available scientific information regarding foundry activities that may benefit from implementing ergonomic solutions.

The general information in this publication is intended to provide foundry employers and workers with effective and practical solutions. It also aims to be a useful reference source when determining the need for ergonomic assistance for specific jobs, such as melting, mold preparation, casting, shakeout and core knockout, and cleaning and cut off. The recommendations and information presented here are intended to be a flexible framework to be adapted to the needs and resources of each individual foundry.

The solutions recommended in this publication may also be beneficial in other industries, such as those that handle heavy materials, use tools for multiple processes, and work on parts of widely varying sizes and shapes (3).

OSHA realizes that some foundries, particularly small ones, may need assistance with certain ergonomic solutions. This may include developing and implementing an ergonomic process or tailoring a recommended solution to a specific situation. Therefore, employers are encouraged to take advantage of OSHA's free consultation services to address these needs.

This publication presents ergonomic solutions that are already implemented within some foundries. OSHA recommends that foundries consider these solutions in the context of a broader, systematic process that includes the elements described in this publication. Such a process will make it more likely that any solutions implemented will be both cost-effective and successful in reducing injuries.

This document includes an introduction, a process for protecting workers, solutions that employers can use to help reduce MSDs in foundries, and additional sources of information on ergonomic applications in foundries.

David Michaels, PhD, MPH
Assistant Secretary of Labor for
Occupational Safety and Health

This guidance is advisory in nature and informational in content. It is not a standard or regulation, and it neither creates new legal obligations nor alters existing obligations created by OSHA standards or the *Occupational Safety and Health Act of 1970* (OSH Act.) Pursuant to the OSH Act, employers must comply with safety and health standards and regulations issued and enforced either by OSHA or by an OSHA-approved state plan. In addition, the Act's General Duty Clause, Section 5(a)(1), requires employers to provide their employees with a workplace free from recognized hazards likely to cause death or serious physical harm.

INTRODUCTION

A foundry is a site where castings are made from molten metal, according to an end user's specifications. Foundry work often includes the following processes: creating casting patterns, making and assembling molds, melting and refining the metal, pouring the metal into molds, and cleaning the finished part (i.e., removing adhering sand and redundant metal from the casting) (5).

Numerous potential hazards are present in a foundry work environment. These include both chemical and physical hazards, such as exposure to dust, silica, lead, noise, heat stress, and gases (e.g., nitrogen dioxide, sulfur dioxide, and carbon monoxide) (3, 6, 7). However, this publication addresses only the ergonomics-related risks to which foundry workers are most often exposed. These risk factors include the following:

- Exerting high levels of force to handle or move materials;
- Doing the same or similar tasks repetitively;
- Working in awkward postures;
- Maintaining static (i.e., nonmoving) body postures for long periods;
- Coming in contact with sharp edges that press into the skin; and
- Being exposed to vibrating tools and work surfaces.

Injuries to the low back and upper limbs are common MSDs among foundry workers. These may arise from doing work repetitively or for prolonged time periods, exerting excessive force to move or grip objects, or using vibrating tools such as chipping hammers and hand-held or rotary grinders (1). Early symptoms of MSDs include pain, restricted joint movement, soft tissue swelling, numbness, and tingling. MSDs typically develop gradually, over time, as a result of intensive work (10).

To develop these guidelines, OSHA visited several foundries that formed the NorthEastern Wisconsin Foundry Ergonomics Partnership (NEWFEP) to address ergonomic issues and implement ergonomic solutions. The foundries specialize in different products and represent a broad range of employment (from several dozen to more than a thousand employees). Work-related MSDs were considerably reduced by the Ergonomics Partnership members. These companies also found that the solutions they implemented lowered absenteeism rates, increased worker productivity and efficiency, and improved product quality. Workers reported that by working in a safer and more comfortable work environment, they experienced less fatigue and improved morale (1, 11).

"By promoting good workplace ergonomics we accomplish a cost saving, but on top of that we have shown our employees that we do truly care about them and the quality of lives they have."

John Smith, Ergo team member, ThyssenKrupp Waupaca

A PROCESS FOR PROTECTING WORKERS

For many foundry operations, the number and severity of MSDs resulting from physical overexertion, as well as their associated costs, can be substantially reduced by applying ergonomic principles (9). OSHA recommends that employers develop a process to systematically address ergonomic issues in their work environments and incorporate it into their existing safety and health programs. In fact, many foundries surveyed by OSHA have integrated an ergonomic process into their overall safety and health program (1). To be most effective, the process should be tailored to an individual foundry's operations.

Foundry management should consider the general steps discussed below when establishing and implementing an ergonomic process. It should be noted, however, that each foundry will have different needs and limitations that should be considered when identifying and addressing workplace concerns. Foundries may implement different types of programs and activities and may assign staff from a variety of departments to accomplish the goals of an ergonomic process. Every foundry is unique; thus, the approach taken to incorporate ergonomic solutions within its operations should consider the foundry's size, structure, and culture.

PROVIDING MANAGEMENT SUPPORT

"Ergonomics is a key component of our safety culture, with management and labor working together in developing creative solutions to unique challenges in our die casting business. We have been able to apply many of these best practices elsewhere in our operations as well."

Jim Sutton, Safety Manager, Mercury Marine

A strong commitment by management is critical to the overall success of an ergonomic process (9). In the development stages, OSHA recommends that foundries define clear goals and objectives for the ergonomic process, discuss them with their workers, assign responsibilities to designated staff members, and communicate clearly with the workforce. Management should promote and help establish a joint worker-management ergonomic team, ensure that regular committee meetings are held, and address workers' concerns in a timely manner. A participatory ergonomic approach, where workers are directly involved in worksite assessments, solution development, and implementation is the essence of a successful ergonomic process. The structure of the team will differ, based on a facility's size and its available human resources. An effective ergonomic process requires a sustained effort, the coordination of activities, and the resources necessary to ensure that the objectives of the ergonomic process are met.

An ergonomic process should be viewed as an ongoing function that is incorporated into the daily workings of the facility, the same as safety and production issues, rather than as an individual project. Management should strongly encourage worker involvement in the ergonomic process and in the decisions that affect their safety and health. Employers also should clearly define procedures that encourage workers to present their concerns to management and provide responses to worker input. Many foundries have successfully integrated other workplace strategies along with an ergonomic process into their business operations. One example is the "lean manufacturing" strategy, which focuses on providing "the right material, to the right place, at the right time, in a proper manner" (1, 13). These strategies attempt to eliminate steps in the manufacturing process that add no value, such as "wasted walking" or "wasted motion" to pick up parts. Ergonomics is a good fit with these strategies because ergonomic principles help identify and control activities that detract from worker performance and may lead to MSDs.

INVOLVING WORKERS

"Solving ergonomic problems has become part of our culture at Manitowoc Grey Iron Foundry. Employee involvement and continuous improvement are the cornerstone of our mission."

Robert Peaslee, President, Manitowoc Grey Iron Foundry, Inc.

Workers can identify and provide important information about hazards in their workplaces. Their opinions and suggestions for change also are valuable, particularly in such a difficult and complex work environment. As such, employees should be included in the early stages of planning an ergonomic process. Workers can also assist in the ergonomic process by voicing their concerns and suggestions for reducing exposure to risk factors and by evaluating the changes made as a result of an ergonomic assessment. Workers can participate in other ergonomics-related activities, such as being part of task abatement groups and lean manufacturing teams, or responding to management surveys and questionnaires. They should be encouraged to provide early reports of MSD symptoms related to a job, which can accelerate the job assessment and improvement process, helping to prevent or reduce the progression of symptoms, the development of serious injuries, and subsequent lost-time claims.

Active participation by workers on ergonomics-related issues helps their acceptance of job changes made as a result of an ergonomic assessment and enables a better understanding of ergonomic principles both on and off the job (1, 12).

Workers involved in ergonomics-related activities within their own plant are able to share their experience and ideas with other foundries, thus increasing the dissemination of their successes. For example, the workers who served on the Ergonomics Partnership Committee provided ergonomic abatement recommendations to the Partnership for consideration by other foundry member sites.

PROVIDING TRAINING

Training is an important element in the ergonomic process. It ensures that workers are aware of ergonomics and its benefits, become informed about ergonomics-related concerns in the workplace, and understand the importance of reporting early symptoms of MSDs. Training should be conducted in a manner and language that all workers understand and is best provided by individuals who have experience with ergonomic issues in foundries.

Training prepares workers to actively participate in many aspects of the ergonomics process, including problem identification, solution implementation, and process evaluation. When training is effective the workers will:

- Learn the principles of ergonomics and their applications;
- Learn about the proper use of equipment, tools, and machine controls;
- Use good work practices, including proper lifting techniques;
- Become more aware of work tasks that may lead to pain or injury;
- Recognize early symptoms of MSDs;
- Understand the importance of addressing early indications of MSDs before serious injury develops; and
- Understand foundry procedures for reporting work-related injuries and illnesses, as required by OSHA's injury and illness recording and reporting regulation (29 CFR Part 1904).

Workers will benefit from an orientation and job-specific hands-on training before they begin their tasks, especially on jobs with potential ergonomic risk factors. Workers should also be notified of workplace changes, instructed on using new equipment, and informed about new work procedures.

IDENTIFYING PROBLEMS

An important part of the ergonomic process is a periodic review of the facility, specific workstation designs and work practices, and the overall production process, from an ergonomics perspective. This includes identifying existing problems, which can be obtained from reviewing the company's OSHA 300 injury and illness logs, 301 reports, workers' compensation records, and worker reports of problems. However, a more forward looking approach, to be used in combination with reviewing injury and illness records, is to be *proactive* in identifying potential ergonomic issues that have gone unnoticed or resulted from facility changes, before they result in MSDs.

Observations of workplace conditions and work processes, ergonomic job analyses, workplace surveys, and worker interviews are common proactive methods for identifying ergonomics-related injury risks. Risk factors that may lead to the development of MSDs include:

- **Exerting excessive force** (4) – Using high levels of physical effort to perform a task, such as manually pouring molds or pushing a loaded rack, or to maintain control of equipment or tools, such as breaking risers from castings.
- **Performing the same or similar tasks repetitively** (4) – Performing the same motion or a series of comparable motions frequently or for an extended period of time, such as grinding finished castings.
- **Doing work in awkward postures, or being in the same posture for long periods of time** (4) – Using postures that place stress on the body. Examples include: reaching above the shoulders to load racks; bending forward, to the side, or twisting to lift castings from containers; kneeling or squatting to inspect the core or mold; or staying in one body posture for a prolonged period, such as standing at a grinding machine for an entire shift.
- **Localized pressure into the body** – Having objects press on the body or a specific body part, such as holding a file with a sharp edge or using the hand as a hammer to align parts.
- **Coming in contact with vibrating surfaces** – Using vibrating tools such as sanders, chippers, drills, grinders, or reciprocating saws.
- **Combined exposure to several risk factors** – Being exposed to a combination of several risk factors that may place workers at higher risk for MSDs than exposure to individual risk factors. The risk of MSD injury depends on the frequency the task is performed, the level of required effort, the duration of the task, as well as other factors (8).

Another proactive means of identifying ergonomics-related issues is to observe worker behaviors. For example, are workers making modifications to their tools, equipment, or work area to address potential risk factors; are they shaking their arms and hands; are they rolling their shoulders; or bringing products, such as back belts or wrist braces, into the workplace.

ENCOURAGING AND UTILIZING REPORTS OF INJURIES

Comprehensive injury reporting is important to the success of an ergonomic process. The goal of this effort is to properly assess, diagnose, and treat MSDs that occur in foundry operations. This allows the foundry to correctly identify work areas or specific tasks where injuries frequently occur or are most severe. This information helps direct the activities of the ergonomic team as well as to guide healthcare providers in making return-to-work and light-duty work decisions.

Encouraging and utilizing reports of injuries:

- Reinforces worker training on recognizing MSD symptoms;
- Encourages early reporting of symptoms of MSDs;
- Allows prompt medical evaluations for diagnosis, treatment, and follow-up care;
- Reduces injury severity, the numbers of workers' compensation claims and associated costs, and the likelihood of permanent disability;
- Provides guidance on return-to-work and work-placement restrictions during the healing process;
- Guides job modifications;
- Provides a mechanism to track and trend foundry-wide MSD injuries; and
- Enables assessment of the effectiveness of work changes.

Note: Federal and state laws prohibit discrimination against workers who report a work-related injury or illness [29 U.S.C. 660(c)].

Healthcare professionals are important ergonomic team members. They help injured workers recover more quickly and return to their jobs with appropriate restrictions and less risk for reinjury. It is necessary that these professionals are knowledgeable about foundry operations and work practices. Their knowledge of the facility will allow them to assist the injured worker during the healing process and in post-injury work placement (1).

IMPLEMENTING SOLUTIONS

"The new automated grinders have eliminated the vibration and stress on my wrists and forearms that used to be a problem when we did it the old way on stand grinders. I now go home and my arms don't hurt and I am also cleaner than before."

Dale Faris, Barinder Grinding Operator, Brillion Iron Works, Inc.

There are several types of ergonomic solutions that are not only feasible, but have already been implemented within foundry operations. Examples of these potential improvements are located in the "Solutions" sections of this publication, and they cover both facility-wide recommendations and solutions for specific operations within foundries.

EVALUATING PROGRESS

Established evaluation and corrective action procedures need to be in place to periodically assess the effectiveness of the ergonomic process and to ensure its continuous improvement and long-term success.

As an ergonomic process is first developing, assessments should include:

- Determining whether goals set for the ergonomic process have been met;
- Determining the success of the implemented ergonomic solutions;
- Evaluating whether:
  o The time between hazard identification and implementation of appropriate solutions has been reduced
  o The number of jobs analyzed and risk factors reduced or eliminated has increased
  o More workers have been trained on ergonomics

- Reviewing facility first-aid reports, absenteeism rates, job transfer requests, or other similar indicators to determine if ergonomics-related efforts have had an immediate impact;
- Obtaining feedback from workers, supervisors, and involved healthcare professionals regarding such issues as any change in their understanding of ergonomics, their enthusiasm or acceptance of the facility's ergonomic process, and worker's attitudes toward their own safety and well-being; and
- Discussing how the ergonomic process should be improved.

For small foundries, the success of an ergonomic process might best be based on interactions with workers and observations of the work environment. A more formal evaluation, including measuring activities and outcome measures to indicate process performance, may be needed for larger foundries. For more established ergonomics processes, evaluations should focus on long-term trends, such as changes in:

- The numbers of OSHA-recordable MSDs or the facility's MSD incidence rate;
- Workers' compensation claims and the average workers' compensation costs per MSD; and
- Medical costs associated with work-related MSDs.

Facilities can use the findings from an ergonomic process evaluation to modify process goals, establish new priorities, and justify the existence of the process.

SOLUTIONS

Many foundries have successfully implemented ergonomic solutions in their facilities as a way to address their workers' MSD injury risks. These interventions have included purchasing new equipment or modifying existing equipment, making changes in work practices, and purchasing new tools or other devices to assist in the production process. Making these changes has reduced the physical demands of foundry work, eliminated unnecessary movements, lowered injury rates and their associated workers' compensation costs, and reduced employee turnover. In many cases, work efficiency and productivity have increased as well (1).

The ergonomic solutions presented in this publication have already been implemented in several foundries. These suggested improvements are not intended to address all ergonomic challenges that foundries face, nor does OSHA expect that every solution presented here will be applicable to each foundry. OSHA recommends that employers first consider using engineering controls, where feasible, to address foundry-related ergonomic issues.

OSHA recognizes that implementing engineering solutions may present certain challenges within a foundry environment, which often involves work that has been performed in a similar way for decades. However, foundry personnel are encouraged to use the examples in this document as a starting point for developing innovative solutions tailored to the specific ergonomic challenges in their individual facilities.

These solutions are grouped according to the jobs to which they most frequently apply:

FACILITY-WIDE SOLUTIONS

MELTING SOLUTIONS

MOLD PREPARATION SOLUTIONS

CASTING SOLUTIONS

SHAKEOUT AND CORE KNOCKOUT SOLUTIONS

CLEANING AND HANDLING SOLUTIONS

FACILITY-WIDE SOLUTIONS

Hoists/Balancers to Transfer Heavy Loads

Before	After

Description:
Devices (powered or non-powered) used to lift and reposition heavy objects

Advantages:
- Replace manual handling of heavy objects
- Reduce the manual force needed to lift and position heavy objects or tools throughout the work area
- Reduce fatigue from frequent lifting

Notes:
- Workers must be trained on proper hoist/balancer use
- Safer hoist/balancer use may initially slow down transfer time
- Several hoist control design trials may be needed before finding the one that works most effectively
- Many makes and models of hoists/balancers are commercially available (e.g., pneumatic, electric, or computer controlled)
- Powered hoists/balancers:
  - Are much more efficient than chain pulls
  - Eliminate manual pulling on a chain
  - Reduce repetitive arm motions
  - Reduce extended arm and shoulder movements
  - Require more workplace setup than non-powered units
- Ensure the hoist is rated for the load weight
- Implement polices requiring hoist use when transferring loads that exceed a set weight limit (e.g., 50 lbs.)

Reduce lifting, pushing, and pulling forces

FACILITY-WIDE SOLUTIONS

Powered Trolleys or Roller Conveyors

Description:
Systems that use mechanical means to transfer heavy or hot items from one location to another

Advantages:
- Minimize forceful pushing, pulling, and carrying
- Move workers farther away from high heat areas or dangerous pinch points

Notes:
- Gravity-fed conveyors may also assist with transfers but will require more handling and effort by workers
- May require a rearrangement of surrounding work areas
- Design should not introduce a trip hazard or contact injuries

Reduce manual pushing of materials

FACILITY-WIDE SOLUTIONS

Lift Tables	Before	After

Description:
Devices used to raise or lower the height of materials for easier handling

Advantages:
- Vertically adjust materials to minimize bending and keep the load close to the body
- Help keep neutral body posture
- May reduce task cycle time
- May increase productivity

Notes:
- A wide variety of lift tables with different features are available:
  - Tables on springs or inflatable bladders that automatically adjust height; good when the weight of items is consistent
  - Power tables, which allow the operator to raise and lower materials as needed; better when the weight of items handled varies
  - Platforms that tilt
  - Platforms that rotate

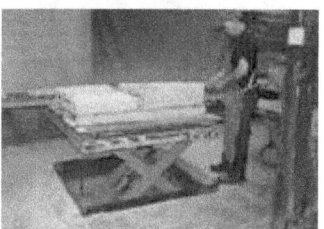

- If bins are used on lift tables, they should have drop-down sides to improve access to items near the bottom of the bin
- The rotating platform feature is especially useful to reach materials that are located near walls or other obstacles

- Lift tables can be installed directly into the floor
- Floor mounted cylinder-like pneumatic lifts can be used to raise carts and pallets

Reduce bending, reaching and walking

FACILITY-WIDE SOLUTIONS

Tilters	Before	After

Description:
Mechanical devices that lift and tilt to adjust materials for easier handling

Advantages:
- Move the load closer to the worker, which reduces extended reaches
- Reduce the forward bending required to handle castings
- May increase productivity

Notes:
- Tilting features minimize access restrictions caused by bin sides
- Workers will require training on using the powered device to lift/tilt heavy containers (e.g., with scrap and ingots)

Reduce bending and reaching

FACILITY-WIDE SOLUTIONS

Modifications of Work Heights to Raise Workers to More Comfortable Heights

Description:
Continuously adjustable elevation of workers to more comfortable heights

Advantage:
- Reduce the amount of above-shoulder reaching required to do work

Notes:
- Any height adjustments should consider both the facility's workforce and the products being manufactured
- Precautions should be taken to make certain that trip hazards are not created

Reduce reaching

FACILITY-WIDE SOLUTIONS

Permanently Raised Standing Work Areas

Description:
Modification of the work surface to raise the worker

Advantages:
- Allow workers to work at their preferred height
- Allow working in a neutral body posture
- Eliminate or reduce extended reaching in front of the body
- Provide stability
- May be made in-house using inexpensive materials

Notes:
- The platform should not present a trip or fall hazard
- Should be implemented in locations where shorter workers must work with raised arms
- In areas where multiple people work, the portable platform should be easily removed and replaced

Reduce awkward body postures

FACILITY-WIDE SOLUTIONS

Platforms or Stack of Pallets to Increase the Height at Which Items are Handled

| Before | After |

Description:
A permanently raised area or stacks of pallets that serve as a low-cost replacement for lift tables

Advantages:
- Allow workers to work in a more upright position
- Reduce the amount of bending by workers
- Reduce forward reach distance
- May shorten task time
- May increase productivity
- Are less expensive than lift tables

Notes:
- This solution works best when work height does not change
- This solution is not practical if workers are exposed to above-shoulder reaching
- Pallets should be in good condition to provide a stable working surface
- Changing work height by adding or removing pallets may be time-consuming
- Pallets are heavy and difficult to handle manually

Reduce bending and reaching

FACILITY-WIDE SOLUTIONS

Height-Appropriate Work Surfaces

Description:
Work tables and benches that can be easily raised or lowered to accommodate workers of different heights

Advantage:
- Reduce awkward working postures of the arms and trunk

Notes:
- For proper height adjustment, workers should focus on the height of the work being done, not the height of the work surface
- If a workstation is shared, height adjustment should be possible without the use of special tools or devices
- If a workstation is used primarily by a single worker, hand cranks or motors for rapid adjustment may not be necessary

Reduce awkward body postures

FACILITY-WIDE SOLUTIONS

Fixtures that Rotate Parts during Production

Description:
Devices that allow parts to be easily turned in multiple directions

Advantages:
- Are adjustable for varying work processes on the same part or for differing work preferences
- Introduce more flexibility for performing tasks
- Reduce extended reaching and awkward postures

Notes:
- This solution may be limited to smaller or lighter-weight items
- The loading and unloading of parts onto the fixture may impact work cycle time
- Make sure that the fixtures are stable and that they prevent unintended movement or rotation of the parts

Reduce reaching and awkward postures

Cut-Outs in Work Tables

Description:
Modified work surfaces to allow workers to perform tasks more easily

Advantages:
- Reduce the reach needed for handling parts, tools, and equipment

Notes:
- The cut-out should not create sharp edges
- The width and depth of the cut-out depends on the locations of parts and tools being handled
- This solution should be considered only if the removed space does not limit the needed working space

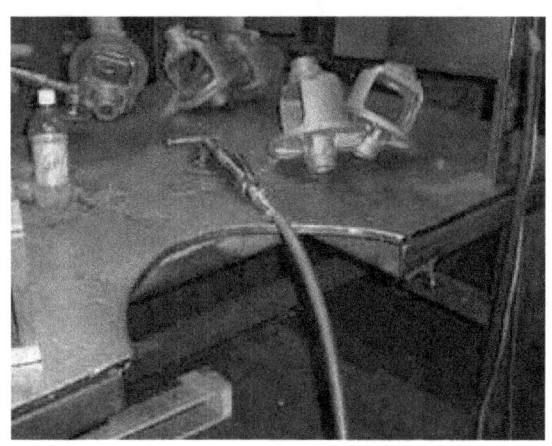

Reduce reaching distances

FACILITY-WIDE SOLUTIONS

Powered Dollies	**Before**	**After**

Description:
Worker-controlled, motorized devices to move loads

Advantages:
* Require less manual effort to push/pull loads
* Shorten task time
* May increase productivity

Notes:
* Many types of dollies are commercially available
* Consider dolly features that allow it to be used for the:
  o Heaviest loads
  o Frequently moved loads
* Powered dollies may be especially useful when loads must be moved up or down ramps or when loads are moved long distances

Reduce physical effort

FACILITY-WIDE SOLUTIONS

Systems to signal the location of materials that need to be moved using powered equipment	Before	After

Description:
A signaling method, which uses lights installed at the end of each workstation. These lights turn on to alert forklift drivers that racks/carts need to be moved

Advantages:
- Reduce the amount of manual pushing and pulling
- Reduce the amount of forklift traffic

Notes:
- Workers should receive training to learn how to use the alert system most effectively
- An inefficient system may impact productivity

Reduce the amount of manual pushing and pulling

FACILITY-WIDE SOLUTIONS

Sit-Stand Stools	Before	After

Description:
Devices that workers can lean against, which are taller than chairs

Advantages:
- Reduce fatigue
- Allow workers at standing workstations to easily change their work postures (e.g., from standing to leaning on stool)
- Workers can get closer to the work since space for the knees is not required
- Promote more comfortable body posture and reduce extended reaches
- Improve blood circulation
- Are relatively low cost

Notes:
- Most sit-stand stools are height-adjustable to meet the needs of workers of varying heights
- Sit-stand stool supports differ by manufacturer; ensure that those used provide stability
- Must ensure that stools are stable, so they do not scoot out from under workers when they sit; casters cannot be used

Reduce fatigue and extended reaches

FACILITY-WIDE SOLUTIONS

Floor Mats in Areas Where Workers Stand for Long Periods of Time

Before	After

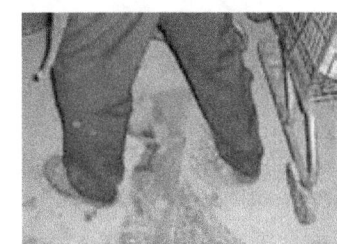

Description:
Cushioned material that softens hard standing surfaces

Advantages:
- Reduce worker fatigue
- Improve overall worker comfort

Notes:
- Provide beveled edge mats to eliminate a trip or fall hazard
- Secure the mats in place
- Regularly clean around and under floor mats
- Replace worn out mats
- Care must be taken where sparks or hot metal may fall on cushioning material
- Selection of the floor mats should be made in accord with industry specifications and standards

Reduce fatigue and discomfort

FACILITY-WIDE SOLUTIONS

Grabbers to Handle Full Barrels

Description:
Mechanical devices, usually attached to fork trucks, that can move and manipulate full barrels

Advantages:
* Reduce the physical demands required to perform tasks
* Minimize the chance of dropping or spilling

Note:
* Workers need to be trained on proper use of the grabbers

Reduce physical effort

Handles or Hand Grip Materials on Tools that are Difficult to Hold

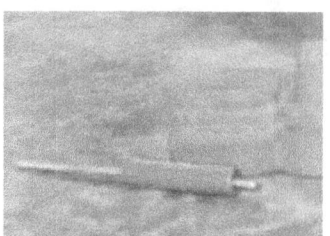

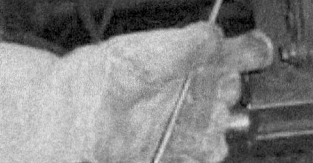

Description:
Handles or material added to tools that form a secure and comfortable grip

Advantages:
* Added handle or material makes tool gripping and manipulating easier
* Reduce use of forceful pinch grips

Note:
* The added handle material may wear out and may need to be replaced periodically

Improve tool grip

MELTING SOLUTIONS

Mechanical Devices to Dump Raw Materials into Top-Loading Furnace

Description:
Handling system to assist with top-loading furnaces

Advantages:
- Reduce the manual handling of materials and the physical demands
- Eliminate manual lifting and tossing of materials
- Reduce back and shoulder injuries
- Reduce exposure to heat
- Minimize the potential for hand contusions, fractures, and burns
- May increase productivity

Note:
- Equipment costs may be recouped in one year or less

Reduce lifting forces, fatigue, and exposure to heat

Mechanical Devices to Load Materials into Furnace

Description:
Handling system with a pneumatic ram to feed ingots into side-loading furnaces

Advantages:
- Reduce the manual handling of materials and the physical demands
- Eliminate manual lifting and tossing of materials
- Reduce back and shoulder injuries
- Reduce exposure to heat
- Minimize the potential for hand contusions, fractures, and burns
- May increase productivity

Notes:
- Materials may still need to be loaded manually onto the device
- Equipment costs may be recouped in one year or less

Before **After**

Reduce fatigue and exposure to heat

MOLD PREPARATION SOLUTIONS

"Lazy Susan" Type Turntable Systems for Inspecting and Finishing Cores

Description:
A device that allows cores to be easily inspected and finished during the work process

Advantages:
- Reduce the amount of force to repeatedly move the cores
- Reduce physical demands on worker's hands/wrist and shoulders
- Can reduce the number of times a core is lifted for finishing and inspection
- Can place the part closer to the worker
- Allow work on the entire circumference of the core without having to reposition the core
- Core can be viewed from different sides without manipulating
- May improve productivity

Notes:
- May take up a lot of floor space
- Ensure that the design of the turntable is load rated for the cores being handled

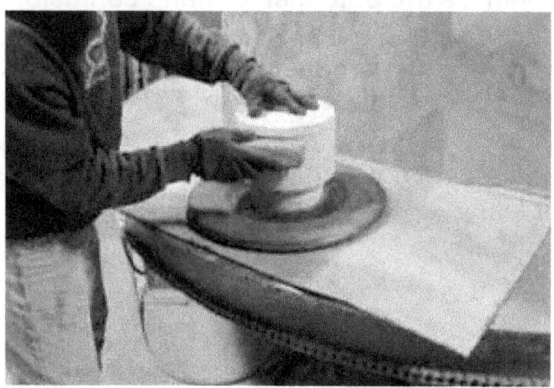

Reduce physical exertions, awkward postures, and reaching

MOLD PREPARATION SOLUTIONS

Shorter and Wider Product Storage Racks

Description:
Shorter and wider racks to improve access to the molds

Advantages:
- Reduce overhead reaching
- Reduce extended forward reaching

Notes:
- Redesigned racks should hold the same amount of molds as those racks being replaced
- Redesigned racks may need more storage space
- Introduce an administrative control rack loading policy to minimize the use of long reach distances to place products on the rack shelves

Reduce awkward postures and extended reaching

Rack Shelves with Roller Wheels

Description:
Rack shelves with integrated roller wheels to reduce force needed to pull patterns out of storage racks. The patterns rest on wheels instead of a shelf surface so they "roll" out of the racks instead of "sliding" out of the racks.

Advantages:
- Rollers reduce the push/pull forces required to drag heavy patterns over the shelves
- Workers have better access to patterns during transport

Notes:
- Retrofit existing racks or install new racks
- Roller mechanisms should be regularly maintained to ensure push/pull forces are minimized
- Ensure that the rack shelves are rated for the load weight

Before	After

Reduce physical exertion

MOLD PREPARATION SOLUTIONS

Automatic Molding Machine

Description:
Machine to join mold halves together

Advantages:
- Reduces awkward postures and pinching hazards associated with moving, flipping and joining mold halves together
- Substantially reduces the amount of physical effort needed to lift and carry molds
- May improve productivity and quality

Notes:
- This system may require reconfiguration of the work area
- Automation requires machine guarding and development of hazardous energy control procedures

Reduces physical exertion and awkward postures

Hoists to Dip Cores

Description:
Overhead systems to lift and lower cores during handling

Advantages:
- Reduce the physical effort required to lift and lower cores
- May improve productivity

Notes:
- Hoist may require a customized hook or device to attach to each core
- Hoist priority should be given to the heaviest cores or those with greater production runs
- Ensure that the hoist is rated for the load weight

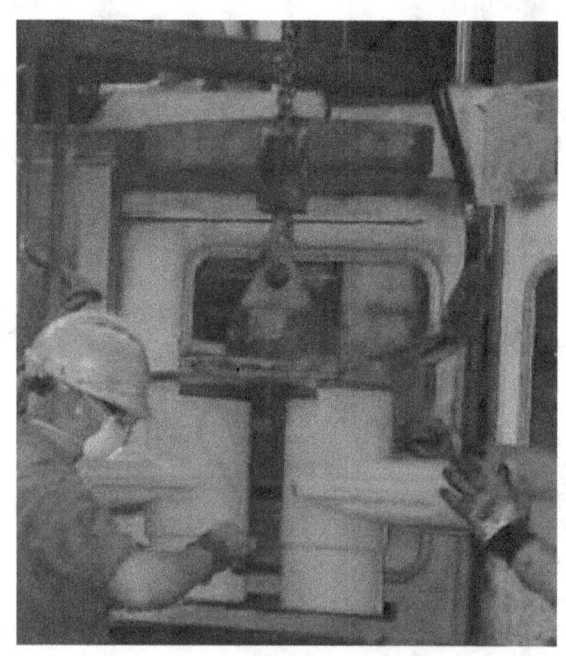

Reduce physical exertions

MOLD PREPARATION SOLUTIONS

Grab Bar on Hook Used to Remove Mold from Core

Description:
Grab bar added to the handling hook, which provides better mechanical support to disengage mold from the core when using an overhead hoist

Advantages:
- Allows workers to use a more secured grip while removing mold from core
- Provides greater control of the hoisted material
- May increase productivity

Notes:
- Grab bar should be oriented so the hand/wrist is in a neutral position
- Hook/grab bar designs may need to be customized for the parts
- Grab bar design should consider wrist posture and pinch points

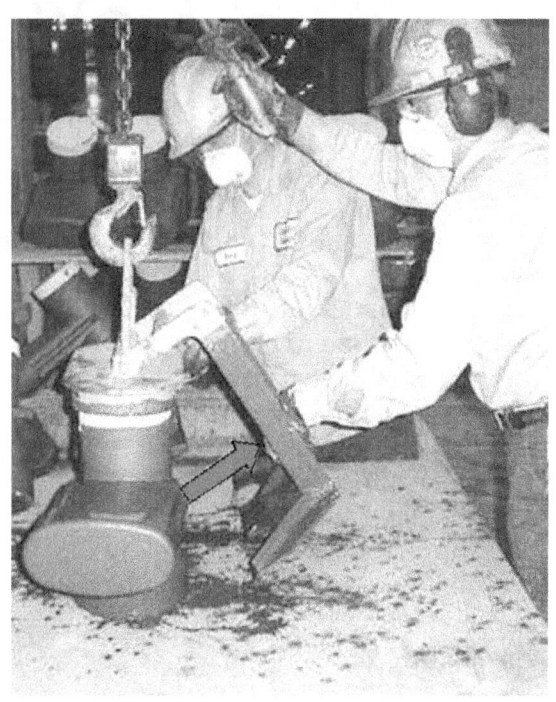

Allows for more controlled gripping

MOLD PREPARATION SOLUTIONS

Motorized Hand Carts for Racks

Description:
Worker-controlled, powered devices that mechanically maneuver heavy, wheeled carts or racks

Advantages:
* Reduce the manual force needed to push/pull wheeled carts
* Reduce back and shoulder injuries
* Reduce travel time to perform task
* May improve productivity

Notes:
* Many types of powered hand carts are commercially available
* Priority should be given to frequently moved racks or racks moved over long distances
* Commercial motorized hand carts may need to be customized

Before	After

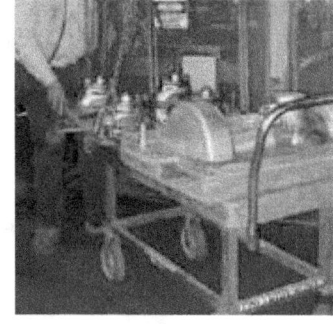	

Reduce physical effort

Lifting Devices to Remove Jacket Sleeves

Description:
Mechanical methods to remove sleeves from molds

Advantages:
* Reduce physical demands on the back and shoulders
* Reduce back and shoulder injuries
* May increase productivity

Note:
* The cost to implement may be recouped in two weeks since a two-man job can now be accomplished by a single worker

Before	After

Reduce physical exertion and awkward posture

MOLD PREPARATION SOLUTIONS

Handles Added to Mold Weights

Description:
Hand grips on weights used on molds as they cool. The old weights were simply metal plates, which were difficult to lift and place on molds.

Advantages:
- Reduce the amount of bending needed to reach weights
- Make moving weights easier, because the handle allows workers to use a comfortable power grip

Notes:
- Handles for the weights can be made in-house
- Ensure that handle openings are wide enough to fit gloved hands

Reduce bending and improve power grip

MOLD PREPARATION SOLUTIONS

Pistol Grip Air Guns to Clean the Mold Patterns

Description:
Right-angle shaped tools with a trigger to activate air flow in a horizontal direction

Advantage:
*   Reduce the awkward positioning of hand/wrist when performing task

Notes:
*   The shape or orientation of the mold being cleaned may determine the appropriate air gun
*   Using an overhead balancer to hang the air gun can further reduce the physical effort

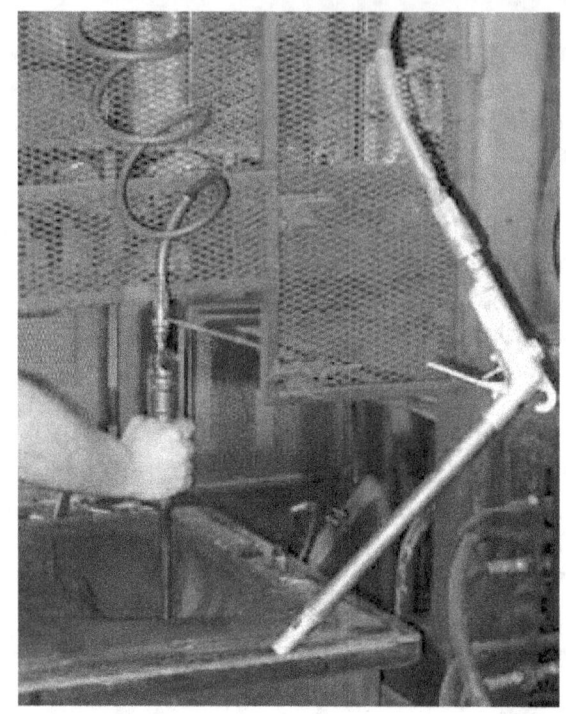

Reduce awkward hand/wrist postures

Inline Drills to Establish Vent Holes in Mold Patterns

Description:
Tools with trigger bars aligned in the activation direction

Advantages:
*   Promote neutral wrist posture by reducing bending of the wrist
*   Neutral wrist posture makes it easier to exert the necessary force

Notes:
*   The best application of the tool is for horizontal work surfaces
*   Using an overhead balancer to hang the air gun can further reduce the physical effort required for the task

Reduce bending of the hand/wrist

CASTING SOLUTIONS

Ceramic Ladles	Before	After

Description:
Ceramic ladles, which are lighter than iron ladles

Advantages:
- Lighter-weight ceramic ladles are easier to lift
- Reduce physical exertion of the back and arms

Notes:
- The cost of ceramic ladles is comparable to iron ladles
- The cost of ceramic ladles may be recouped in one day

Reduce physical effort

Balancer Systems to Bear the Weight of the Pot/Ladle	Before	After

Description:
Overhead devices to support the weight of the pouring pot/ladle

Advantages:
- Reduce the physical effort required of operator to perform the task
- Increase the ability to control pouring pot/ladle movement
- Reduce fatigue
- May improve productivity

Notes:
- Balancer systems may be constructed in-house
- Training will need to be provided

Reduce physical exertion

CASTING SOLUTIONS

Powered Devices to Raise and Lower Ladles

Description:
Mechanical equipment to replace using hand wheels to manually reposition ladles

Advantages:
- Reduce repetitive movements of the arms and shoulders
- Reduce the physical demands of ladle handling

Note:
- Controls should be properly located to minimize awkward shoulder positions

Before	After

Reduce physical effort and repetitive movements

Slip-Resistant Ladle-Pouring Handles

Description:
Friction-increasing materials (e.g., grip tape) or modified handles (e.g., knurling) to improve grip

Advantages:
- Increase the control during the ladle-pouring process
- Improve pouring accuracy and reduce spillage
- Reduce the grip force, which must be exerted to turn the wheel

Note:
- Slip-resistant material should cover the entire handling surface and may need to be replaced frequently

Improve grip

CASTING SOLUTIONS

Spout Extensions Used to Fill Ladles

Description:
An extension to the spout on brass furnaces

Advantages:
- Reduce forward reaching needed to move worker away from heat
- Reduce awkward shoulder postures
- Reduce stress on shoulders

Note:
- Ensure that the extension does not produce an impact hazard

Before	After

Reduce forward reaching distance and awkward postures

Rounded Handles on Metal Pouring Ladles

Description:
Ball-shaped handle securely attached to the current lever

Advantages:
- Allow worker to operate ladle using a stronger grip
- Improve operator's control of the pouring ladle
- Eliminate sharp edges that could press into an operator's hands
- May reduce spillage

Note:
- Handle ends could be round or oval in shape to suit the needs of the task and worker preferences

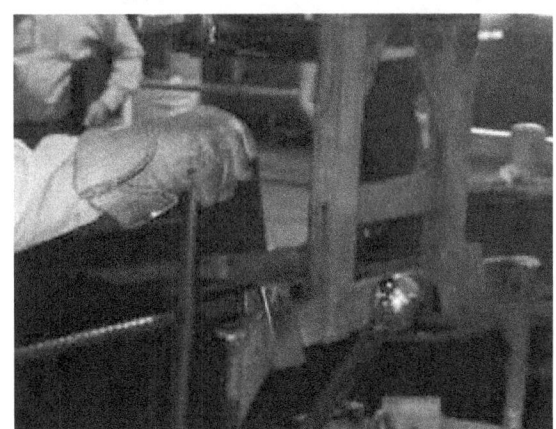

Improve grip and reduce contact stress

CASTING SOLUTIONS

Elevated Platforms along Pour Lines

Description:
Stable platforms to elevate workers while pouring

Advantages:
- Reduce the amount of vertical reaching required to pour molds
- May lower the amount of molten metal spillage

Notes:
- Precautions should be taken to make certain that trip hazards are not created
- If platforms are higher than 4 ft. from the floor, rails should be installed

Reduce over-shoulder reaching

Elevated Locations to Rake Slag

Description:
A raised position where a worker can remove slag from the perimeter of holding tanks

Advantage:
- Reduce overhead or forward reaching

Notes:
- Ensure that any raised positions do not create trip/fall hazards
- Consider how the raised location may impact one's ability to view the task

Reduce reaching

SHAKEOUT AND CORE KNOCKOUT SOLUTIONS

Impactors for Shakeout Work	Before	After

Description:
Mechanical impactors supported by balancers that can remove sand, gating, and metal from castings

Advantages:
- Reduce manual force needed for spruing and eliminate sledge hammer use
- A balancer supports the weight and makes it more maneuverable
- May increase productivity

Note:
- Workers will require training on using impactors/wedges

Reduce physical exertion and fatigue

SHAKEOUT AND CORE KNOCKOUT SOLUTIONS

| Hydraulic, Pressure-Powered Wedges to Remove Risers | Before | After |

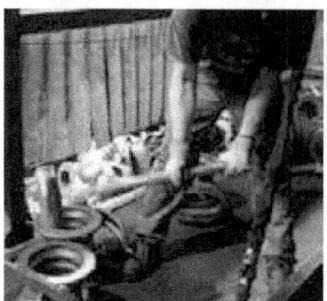

Description:
Mechanical impact tools supported on tool balancers that replace sledgehammers

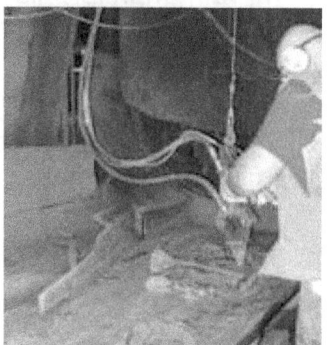

Advantages:
- Reduce awkward shoulder and trunk postures
- Eliminate the forces needed to grasp, swing, and hold sledgehammer
- May reduce task cycle time

Notes:
- Different wedges may be needed for different castings
- Wedges need to be supported on the balancer in the frequently used position

Reduce physical exertion and awkward postures

SHAKEOUT AND CORE KNOCKOUT SOLUTIONS

Mechanical Devices to Open Dies

Description:
Powered equipment to open dies, which replaces manual opening with pry bars

Advantages:
- Eliminate manually prying apart dies
- Reduce body fatigue
- Reduce the amount of awkward postures
- Reduce the risk of burns
- May increase productivity

Note:
- Cost to implement system may be recouped within a few months

Reduce physical exertion and awkward postures

SHAKEOUT AND CORE KNOCKOUT SOLUTIONS

Mechanical Devices to Assist in Core Removal

Description:
Powered devices that support core weights during lifting and transporting between the rack and the shakeout pan

Advantages:
- Reduce the manual handling of cores
- Reduce physical demands on the back and shoulders by eliminating lifting and carrying

Note:
- Workers will need training on proper use of the equipment

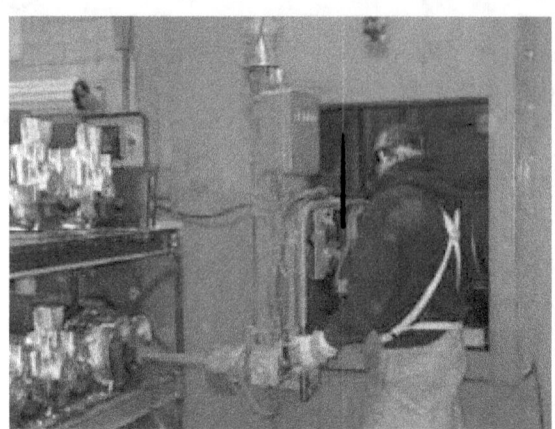

Reduce manual handling and physical exertion

SHAKEOUT AND CORE KNOCKOUT SOLUTIONS

Diverters to Channel the Direction of Castings	Before	After

Description:
A sturdy add-on to shaker tables to guide casting movement towards the worker

Advantage:
- Reduce the extended reaching and torso bending required to access and handle castings

Notes:
- These guides can be installed at little cost
- Diverter may need to be adjustable for castings that differ greatly in size or shape

Reduce reaching

SHAKEOUT AND CORE KNOCKOUT SOLUTIONS

Extension Slide at the Output of Shaker Table to Automatically Drop Parts into Bins

Description:
A modification to existing equipment, which uses gravity to automatically transfer parts

Advantages:
- Eliminates use of repeated hook and pull
- Reduces the handling of castings

Notes:
- Workers may need to monitor bins to prevent overflow of parts
- Defective parts may still need to be handled manually

Reduces physical exertion

SHAKEOUT AND CORE KNOCKOUT SOLUTIONS

Powered Conveyors to Transfer and Dump Molds to Shakeout Pans

Reduce physical exertion

Description:
A motorized method to move molds to shakeout pans

Advantages:
- Eliminate need to manually push molds along the production line
- Reduce the physical demand on the back and shoulders to manually lift molds from conveyor and break them
- Reduce work in awkward body postures
- Reduce fatigue
- Reduce burn risk to workers
- May increase productivity

Notes:
- Existing lines need to be replaced or retrofitted
- Implementation costs may be recouped within six-to-twelve months

Rounded Edges Added to the Sides of Shakeout Lines

Reduce pressure against body

Description:
Smooth surfaces that do not press into workers' bodies when leaning against equipment

Advantage:
- Reduce contact pressure from sharp equipment edges

Notes:
- Ensure that new edges do not extend away from the conveyor resulting in over-extended reaches
- Modifications can be made in-house

CLEANING AND HANDLING SOLUTIONS

Grinders with User-Friendly Features

Description:
Pneumatic tools with task-enhancing features such as vibration dampening properties, lighter weight and more effective grinding heads

Advantages:
- Lighter weight may reduce grinding effort/ fatigue
- Reduce awkward postures of the hands/wrists, elbows, and shoulders during activity
- Improve control over the grinding task
- Reduce exposure to vibration
- May improve access to different areas of the casting
- May take material off faster and improve grinding efficiency, productivity, and quality

Notes:
- New equipment costs may be recouped within four-to-twelve months
- Many newly-designed grinders are commercially available; test different grinding wheels before making a purchasing decision
- Alternative grinder attachments may be placed on currently used grinders (e.g., pads that can grind more rapidly)
- Ensure proper guarding of the wheel on all handheld grinders

Reduce physical exertion and awkward wrist postures

CLEANING AND HANDLING SOLUTIONS

Mechanical Lifts to Move Cast Materials	Before	After

Description:
Hoists that bear the weight of the casting being handled

Advantages:
- Minimize the manual transfer of parts
- Reduce physical stress on back and shoulders
- Reduce whole-body fatigue
- May lower the risk of burns
- May increase productivity

Note:
- Custom attachments may be needed to handle different parts

Reduce manual lifting

CLEANING AND HANDLING SOLUTIONS

Portable Conveyors to Move Materials

Description:
Wheeled portable transfer system that can be readily moved from location to location as needed

Advantages:
* Reduce bending and other awkward postures while handling materials
* Reduce the amount of carrying of material
* May reduce work cycle times
* May improve productivity

Notes:
* Portable conveyors that incline can further reduce the manual handling of materials by allowing transport to different elevations
* Consider floor surface and load weight when selecting wheels for conveyors

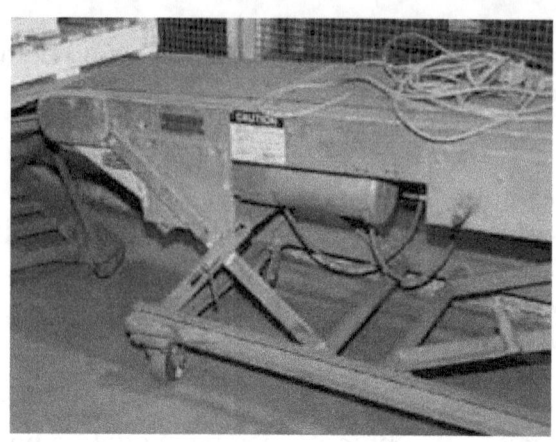

Reduce physical exertion and awkward postures

CLEANING AND HANDLING SOLUTIONS

Automated Casting Trim and Finishing

Description:
Powered machines to replace hand or stand grinders for finishing work

Advantages:
- Minimize grinder usage and exposure to hand/arm vibration
- Decrease the time operators must work while looking down
- Reduce manual parts handling
- Reduce task cycle times
- Minimize potential exposure to flying debris and airborne metal contamination
- Improve product quality and consistency
- Reduce noise levels
- In some cases, can eliminate need for a ventilation helmet
- May improve productivity

Note:
- Implementation costs may be recouped within one year

Reduce exposure to vibration and awkward postures

CLEANING AND HANDLING SOLUTIONS

Automated Finishing Equipment

Description:
Automated equipment to replace hand grinders and finishing tools

Advantages:
- Eliminates grinder use and exposure to hand/ arm vibration
- Improves operator work posture
- Serves as a barrier to protect operators from flying debris and sparks
- Controls noise from process
- Improves product quality and scheduling

Notes:
- Equipment may require more floor space
- Ensure that parts loading and unloading does not require extended reaching

Reduces physical exertions

Presses to Assemble Parts

Description:
Mechanical presses to set parts instead of using manual pounding

Advantages:
- Reduce physical effort required for manual pounding
- Eliminate use of hand tools

Notes:
- Presses may be designed and made in-house
- May improve parts quality and reduce scrap
- Individual presses may be needed for each type of part produced

Before

After

Reduce force

CLEANING AND HANDLING SOLUTIONS

Fixtures to Affix Parts

Description:
Fixture to automatically insert and affix clamps, and position castings on forging tools, which replaces manual power with machine power

Advantages:
- Reduce physical demands on workers' hands/wrists and shoulders
- Utilizes mechanical force instead of muscle force
- May improve productivity

Notes:
- A customized fixture may be needed for each assembled part
- Implementation costs may be recouped within one month
- Consider creating a fixture that can position the casting in various orientations

Before	After
	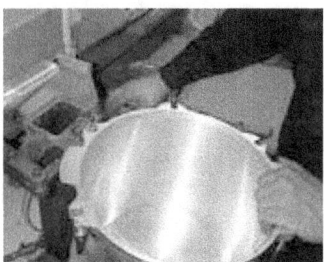
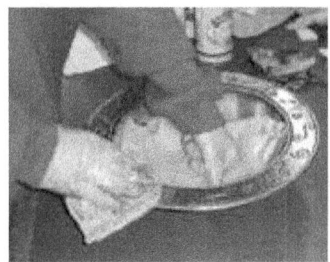	

Reduce physical exertions

Powered Drivers to Assemble Components

Description:
Pneumatic or electric tools that replace hand tools for assembling finished parts

Advantages:
- Reduce repetition and awkward postures to the hands/wrists and shoulders
- Improve productivity

Note:
- Implementation cost may be recouped within one week

Before	After

Reduce physical exertion, repetition and awkward postures

CLEANING AND HANDLING SOLUTIONS

Box-Taping Machines

Before | **After**

Description:
Equipment that automatically tapes boxes containing finished castings

Advantages:
- Reduce physical demands required to staple boxes manually
- Reduce awkward postures during finished castings packing
- Produce a higher quality shipping container
- May improve productivity

Reduce physical exertion

Notes:
- Worker will need to be trained on using the machine
- Implementation cost may be recouped within one month

Plastic-Wrap Machines to Enclose Materials

Description:
Automatic means of wrapping pallets of finished product

Advantages:
- Substantially reduce the amount of physical effort to wrap finished product manually
- Reduce awkward postures and extended reaching
- May increase productivity

Note:
- The machine will require more floor space

Reduce physical effort and awkward postures

ADDITIONAL SOURCES OF INFORMATION

The following sources may be useful to those seeking further information about ergonomics and the prevention of work-related MSDs in foundries.

- *Elements of Ergonomics Programs*, U.S. Department of Health and Human Services, National Institute for Occupational Safety and Health, (NIOSH), Publication # 97-117, 1997, http://www.cdc.gov/niosh/docs/97-117. The document describes the basic elements of a workplace program aimed at preventing work-related MSDs. It includes a "toolbox," which is a collection of techniques, methods, reference materials, and sources for other information that can help in program development.

- Many states and territories operate their own occupational safety and health programs under plans approved by Federal OSHA. Information on specific state foundry initiatives and compliance assistance, as well as state standards that may apply to foundries is available on OSHA's website at: www.osha.gov/dcsp/osp/index.html.

- Free On-site Consultation Services for Small Business. OSHA's On-site Consultation Program offers free and confidential advice to small and medium-sized businesses in all states across the country, with priority given to high-hazard worksites. On-site consultation services are separate from enforcement and do not result in penalties or citations. Consultants from state agencies or universities work with employers to identify workplace hazards, provide advice on compliance with OSHA standards, and assist in establishing safety and health management programs.

    For more information, to find the local On-site Consultation office in your state, or to request a brochure on Consultation Services, visit http://www.osha.gov/dcsp/smallbusiness/consult.html, or call 1-800-321-OSHA [6742].

- Seven foundries in OSHA's Region V formed the NorthEastern Wisconsin Foundry Ergonomics Partnership to address ergonomic hazards in a foundry setting. This initiative reduced injury and illness rates, increased awareness of ergonomic risk among workers and management, and significantly increased productivity and/or reduced workers' compensation costs. More information on the Partnership's successes can be found at: https://www.osha.gov/dcsp/success_stories/partnerships/region5/261_fep_success.html.

- Through their Alliance (http://www.osha.gov/dcsp/alliances/afs/afs.html), OSHA and the American Foundry Society (AFS) encourage AFS members and others, including small businesses, in the metalcasting industry to increase worker access to safety and health information and training resources on workplace issues. AFS provides and promotes knowledge and services that strengthen the metalcasting industry for the ultimate benefit of its customers and society.

REFERENCES

(1) Reports of OSHA site visits to foundries.

(2) Bureau of Labor Statistics. U.S. Department of Labor, November 2011.

(3) Ramsey, J., J. Eisenberg. 2008. Ergonomic Evaluation of Workers at a Piston and Cylinder Liner Manufacturing Plant. *NIOSH Health Hazard Evaluation Report HETA 2007-0124-3060.*

(4) Da Costa, B.R., E. R. Vieira. 2010. Risk factors for work-related musculoskeletal disorders: A systematic review of recent longitudinal studies. *American Journal of Industrial Medicine,* Vol. 53, pp. 285-323.

(5) Steel Founders' Society of America at: http://www.sfsa.org/sfsa/cstintcp.php.

(6) Armstrong, T. J., M. M. Marshall, B. J. Martin, J. A. Foulke, D. C. Grieshaber, G. Malon. 2002. Exposure to forceful exertions and vibration in a foundry. *International Journal of Industrial Ergonomics,* Vol. 30, Issue 3, pp. 163-179.

(7) Muzammil, M., A. Ali Khan. 2007. Effect of noise, heat stress and exposure duration on operators in a die casting operation. *Occupational Ergonomics,* Vol. 7, No. 4, pp. 233-245.

(8) Musculoskeletal Disorders and Workplace Factors – A Critical Review of Epidemiologic Evidence for Work-Related Musculoskeletal Disorders of the Neck, Upper Extremity and Low Back. 1997. U.S. Department of Health and Human Services. National Institute for Occupational Safety and Health (NIOSH), Publication No. 97-141.

(9) National Research Council and Institute of Medicine. 2001. Musculoskeletal Disorders and the Workplace – Low Back and Upper Extremities. National Academy of Sciences. Washington, DC: National Academy Press.

(10) Hoozenmans, M.J.M., A. J. van der Beek, M. H. W. Frings-Dresen, L. H. V. van der Woude, F. J. H. van Dijk. 2002. Pushing and pulling in association with low back and shoulder complaints. *Occupational and Environmental Medicine* 59, pp. 696-702.

(11) https://www.osha.gov/dcsp/success_stories/partnerships/region5/261_fep_success.html.

(12) Marras, W.S. 2000. Occupational low back disorder causation and control. *Ergonomics.* Vol. 43, No. 7, pp. 880-902.

(13) Butt, S.E., T. K. Fredericks, S. Amin-Kumar, S. Ramrattan. 2009, Safety and Ergonomics Revisited: How has the Industry Changed in 10 Years? No. 09-115, *Transactions,* American Foundry Society, Vol. 117, pp. 847-856.

OSHA offers free compliance assistance to employers and workers. Several OSHA programs and services can help employers identify and correct job hazards, as well as improve their injury and illness prevention program.

Establishing an Injury and Illness Prevention Program

The key to a safe and healthful work environment is a comprehensive injury and illness prevention program.

Injury and illness prevention programs are systems that can substantially reduce the number and severity of workplace injuries and illnesses, while reducing costs to employers. Thousands of employers across the United States already manage safety using illness and injury prevention programs, and OSHA believes that all employers can and should do the same. Thirty-four states have requirements or voluntary guidelines for workplace injury and illness prevention programs. Most successful injury and illness prevention programs are based on a common set of key elements. These include management leadership, worker participation, hazard identification, hazard prevention and control, education and training, and program evaluation and improvement. Visit OSHA's illness and injury prevention program web page at www.osha.gov/dsg/topics/safetyhealth for more information.

Compliance Assistance Specialists

OSHA has compliance assistance specialists throughout the nation located in most OSHA offices. Compliance assistance specialists can provide information to employers and workers about OSHA standards, short educational programs on specific hazards or OSHA rights and responsibilities, and information on additional compliance assistance resources. For more details, visit http://www.osha.gov/dcsp/compliance_assistance/index.html or call 1-800-321-OSHA [6742] to contact your local OSHA office.

Free On-site Consultation Services for Small Business

OSHA's On-site Consultation Program offers free and confidential advice to small and medium-sized businesses in all states across the country, with priority given to high-hazard worksites.

Each year, responding to requests from small employers looking to create or improve their safety and health management programs, OSHA's On-site Consultation Program conducts over 29,000 visits to small business worksites covering over 1.5 million workers across the nation.

On-site consultation services are separate from enforcement and do not result in penalties or citations. Consultants from state agencies or universities work with employers to identify workplace hazards, provide advice on compliance with OSHA standards, and assist in establishing safety and health management programs.

For more information, to find the local On-site Consultation office in your state, or to request a brochure on Consultation Services, visit http://www.osha.gov/dcsp/smallbusiness/consult.html, or call 1-800-321-OSHA [6742].

Under the consultation program, certain exemplary employers may request participation in OSHA's **Safety and Health Achievement Recognition Program (SHARP)**. Eligibility for participation includes, but is not limited to, receiving a full-service, comprehensive consultation visit, correcting all identified hazards and developing an effective safety and health management program. Worksites that receive SHARP recognition are exempt from programmed inspections during the period that the SHARP certification is valid.

Cooperative Programs

OSHA offers cooperative programs under which businesses, labor groups and other organizations can work cooperatively with OSHA. To find out more about any of the following programs, visit http://www.osha.gov/dcsp/compliance_assistance/index_programs.html.

Alliance Program

Through the Alliance Program, OSHA works with groups committed to worker safety and health to prevent workplace fatalities, injuries and illnesses. These groups include trade or professional organizations, employers, unions, consulates, faith-

and community-based organizations and educational institutions. OSHA and the groups work together to develop compliance assistance tools and resources, share information with workers and employers, and educate workers and employers about their rights and responsibilities.

OSHA Strategic Partnership Program (OSPP)

The OSPP provides the opportunity for OSHA to partner with employers, workers, professional or trade associations, labor organizations, and/or other interested stakeholders. OSHA Strategic Partnerships (OSP) are formalized through unique agreements designed to encourage, assist, and recognize partner efforts to eliminate serious hazards and achieve model workplace safety and health practices.

Challenge Program

OSHA Challenge provides interested employers and workers the opportunity to gain assistance in improving their safety and health management programs. OSHA Challenge is available to general industry, maritime and construction employers in the private and public sectors under OSHA's federal jurisdiction.

Voluntary Protection Programs (VPP)

The VPP recognize employers and workers in private industry and federal agencies who have implemented effective safety and health management programs and maintain injury and illness rates below the national average for their respective industries. In VPP, management, labor, and OSHA work cooperatively and proactively to prevent fatalities, injuries, and illnesses through a system focused on: hazard prevention and control, worksite analysis, training, and management commitment and worker involvement. To participate, employers must submit an application to OSHA and undergo a rigorous on-site evaluation by a team of safety and health professionals. Union support is required for applicants who are represented by a bargaining unit. VPP participants are re-evaluated every three to five years to remain in the programs. VPP participants are exempt from OSHA programmed inspections while they maintain their VPP status.

Occupational Safety and Health Training

The OSHA Training Institute in Arlington Heights, Illinois, provides basic and advanced training and education in safety and health for federal and state compliance officers, state consultants, other federal agency personnel and private sector employers, workers, and their representatives.

In addition, 25 OSHA Training Institute Education Centers at 44 locations throughout the United States deliver courses on OSHA standards and occupational safety and health issues to thousands of students a year.

For more information on training, contact the OSHA Directorate of Training and Education, 2020 Arlington Heights Road, Arlington Heights, IL 60005; call 1-847-297-4810; or visit www.osha.gov.

Susan Harwood Training Grants

OSHA awards grants to nonprofit organizations to provide workers and small employers with safety and health training and education about hazard identification and prevention. Grants focus on small business, hard-to-reach workers and high-hazard industries.

Grantees develop programs that address safety and health topics selected by OSHA, recruit workers and employers for the training and conduct the training. They are also expected to follow up with students to find out how they have applied the training in their workplaces.

For more information on training grants, contact the OSHA Directorate of Training and Education by calling 1-847-297-4810 or visiting www.osha.gov.

OSHA Educational Materials

OSHA has many types of educational materials in English, Spanish, Vietnamese and other languages available in print or online. These include:
- Brochures/booklets that cover a wide variety of job hazards and other topics;
- Fact Sheets, which contain basic background information on safety and health hazards;
- Guidance documents that provide detailed examinations of specific safety and health issues;

- Online Safety and Health Topics pages;
- Posters;
- Small, laminated QuickCards™ that provide brief safety and health information; and
- *QuickTakes*, OSHA's free, twice-monthly online newsletter with the latest news about OSHA initiatives and products to assist employers and workers in finding and preventing workplace hazards. To sign up for *QuickTakes* visit OSHA's website at www.osha.gov and click on *QuickTakes* at the top of the page.

To view materials available online or for a listing of free publications, visit OSHA's website at www.osha.gov. You can also call 1-800-321-OSHA [6742] to order publications.

OSHA's website also has a variety of eTools. These include utilities such as expert advisors, electronic compliance assistance, videos and other information for employers and workers. To learn more about OSHA's safety and health tools online, visit www.osha.gov.

NIOSH HEALTH HAZARD EVALUATION PROGRAM

Getting Help with Health Hazards

The National Institute for Occupational Safety and Health (NIOSH) is a federal agency that conducts scientific and medical research on workers' safety and health. At no cost to employers or workers, NIOSH can help identify health hazards and recommend ways to reduce or eliminate those hazards in the workplace through its Health Hazard Evaluation (HHE) Program.

Workers, union representatives and employers can request a NIOSH HHE. An HHE is often requested when there is a higher than expected rate of a disease or injury in a group of workers. These situations may be the result of an unknown cause, a new hazard, or a mixture of sources. To request a NIOSH Health Hazard Evaluation go to www.cdc.gov/niosh/hhe/request.html. To find out more about the Health Hazard Evaluation Program:
- Call (513) 841-4382, or to talk to a staff member in Spanish, call (513) 841-4439; or
- Send an email to HHERequestHelp@cdc.gov.

OSHA REGIONAL OFFICES

Region I
Boston Regional Office
(CT*, ME, MA, NH, RI, VT*)
JFK Federal Building, Room E340
Boston, MA 02203
(617) 565-9860 (617) 565-9827 Fax

Region II
New York Regional Office
(NJ*, NY*, PR*, VI*)
201 Varick Street, Room 670
New York, NY 10014
(212) 337-2378 (212) 337-2371 Fax

Region III
Philadelphia Regional Office
(DE, DC, MD*, PA, VA*, WV)
The Curtis Center
170 S. Independence Mall West
Suite 740 West
Philadelphia, PA 19106-3309
(215) 861-4900 (215) 861-4904 Fax

Region IV
Atlanta Regional Office
(AL, FL, GA, KY*, MS, NC*, SC*, TN*)
61 Forsyth Street, SW, Room 6T50
Atlanta, GA 30303
(678) 237-0400 (678) 237-0447 Fax

Region V
Chicago Regional Office
(IL*, IN*, MI*, MN*, OH, WI)
230 South Dearborn Street
Room 3244
Chicago, IL 60604
(312) 353-2220 (312) 353-7774 Fax

Region VI
Dallas Regional Office
(AR, LA, NM*, OK, TX)
525 Griffin Street, Room 602
Dallas, TX 75202
(972) 850-4145 (972) 850-4149 Fax
(972) 850-4150 FSO Fax

Region VII
Kansas City Regional Office
(IA*, KS, MO, NE)
Two Pershing Square Building
2300 Main Street, Suite 1010
Kansas City, MO 64108-2416
(816) 283-8745 (816) 283-0547 Fax

Region VIII
Denver Regional Office
(CO, MT, ND, SD, UT*, WY*)
1999 Broadway, Suite 1690
Denver, CO 80202
(720) 264-6550 (720) 264-6585 Fax

Region IX
San Francisco Regional Office
(AZ*, CA*, HI*, NV*, and American Samoa,
Guam and the Northern Mariana Islands)
90 7th Street, Suite 18100
San Francisco, CA 94103
(415) 625-2547 (415) 625-2534 Fax

Region X
Seattle Regional Office
(AK*, ID, OR*, WA*)
300 Fifth Avenue, Suite 1280
Seattle, WA 98104
(206) 757-6700 (206) 757-6705 Fax

* These states and territories operate their own OSHA-approved job safety and health plans and cover state and local government employees as well as private sector employees. The Connecticut, Illinois, New Jersey, New York and Virgin Islands programs cover public employees only. (Private sector workers in these states are covered by Federal OSHA). States with approved programs must have standards that are identical to, or at least as effective as, the Federal OSHA standards.

Note: To get contact information for OSHA area offices, OSHA-approved state plans and OSHA consultation projects, please visit us online at www.osha.gov or call us at 1-800-321-OSHA (6742).

HOW TO CONTACT OSHA

For questions or to get information or advice,
to report an emergency, report a fatality or
catastrophe, order publications, sign up for
OSHA's e-newsletter, or to file a confidential
complaint, contact your nearest OSHA office,
visit www.osha.gov or call OSHA at
1-800-321-OSHA (6742), TTY 1-877-889-5627.

**For assistance, contact us.
We are OSHA. We can help.**